Understandir

PREGNANCY

Elizabeth Fenwick

ublished by Family Doctor Publications
1 association with the British Medical Association

IMPORTANT

This book is intended not as a substitute for personal medical advice but as a supplement to that advice for the patient who wishes to understand more about his or her condition.

Before taking any form of treatment YOU SHOULD ALWAYS CONSULT YOUR MEDICAL PRACTITIONER.

In particular (without limit) you should note that advances in medical science occur rapidly and some of the information about drugs and treatment contained in this booklet may very soon be out of date.

© Family Doctor Publications 1996, 2000, 2001
Reprinted 1998
Second edition 2000
Reprinted 2001

Family Doctor Publications, PO Box 4664, Poole BH15 1NN

Medical Editor: Dr Tony Smith
Consultant Editor: Jane Sugarman
Cover Artist: Dave Eastbury
Medical Artist: Philip Wilson and Debbie Maizels
Design: MPG Design, Blandford Forum, Dorset
Printing: Reflex Litho, Thetford, using acid-free paper

ISBN: 1 898205 96 5

Contents

Planning for pregnancy

Pregnancy and childbirth are now safer than they have ever been, for both mother and baby. Maybe you're pregnant already. But if you are just thinking about becoming pregnant, so much the better. Try to give yourselves three months to prepare for pregnancy. Having a baby is one of the most important things that you will ever do, so it is worth planning ahead to get your baby off to the best possible start.

TALKING TO YOUR DOCTOR

If you have a long-standing disorder such as epilepsy or diabetes, talk to your doctor before trying to become pregnant. If the drugs you have to take might harm your baby or make it harder for you to conceive, your doctor may want to change your treatment in good time.

GIVING UP THE PILL

It can take several months for your periods to become regular again if you have been on the Pill. If you conceive during this time, it will be difficult to predict when your baby is due. So after coming off the Pill, it's best to wait until you have had three normal periods before trying to become pregnant.

SMOKING

Cigarette smoke is a real hazard for your baby, even during pregnancy (see page 18). Smoking can affect fertility too. Try to give up before becoming pregnant if you can.

GERMAN MEASLES

Probably you were immunised against German measles when you were at school. But if you were not, or are not sure, tell your doctor now. If you get the disease during pregnancy it can damage your baby. A blood test will show whether or not you are immune. If you are not, you can be immunised, but this must be done at least three months before you try to become pregnant.

Having a baby is one of the most important things you will ever do, so it is worth planning ahead to get your baby off to the best possible start.

FOLIC ACID

Folic acid is a vitamin that helps prevent neural tube defects (such as spina bifida). Black-eyed beans and fresh, dark-green, leafy vegetables are among the best sources of folic acid, but in the first four weeks of pregnancy you need three times as much folic acid as you would normally eat in one day. It's essential to take a folic acid supplement. Folic acid tablets can be bought over the counter without a prescription, and you need to take 400 micrograms each day.

Start taking it before you start trying to conceive, because it should be taken for at least one week before you become pregnant, and for the first 12 weeks of pregnancy. If you have already had a baby with a spinal cord defect, your doctor will recommend that you take a higher dose (four milligrams) of folic acid daily.

THE BEST AGE FOR PREGNANCY

More and more women nowadays are having their first baby at a later age. Although it is slightly easier for a woman to become pregnant in her twenties, pregnancy and childbirth are perfectly safe for older women, although, in a first pregnancy, they may have a longer labour and a greater chance of a stillbirth. However, how old you are matters less than how healthy you are; for the fit woman with good antenatal care these risks are reduced.

For very young mothers the risks are greater. Babies born to teenagers are smaller, more likely to be premature and more likely to die during the first year of life, probably because the teenager hasn't finished growing and mother and baby compete for nutrients. The very young mother is herself at risk, because her pelvis may not have finished growing and will not be big enough for the baby to pass through.

WORKING WITH HAZARDOUS SUBSTANCES

Your employer has a responsibility to make sure that you are not exposed to any risks at work that might affect your chances of conception, or involve any risk to the baby. At one time it was suggested that it might be dangerous for pregnant women to work with VDUs, but the most recent research shows no evidence for this.

GENETIC COUNSELLING

About two or three children in every 100 born have a serious mental or physical disability.

Sometimes this is because the baby doesn't develop normally during pregnancy, but sometimes the disorder is inherited from one or (more usually) both parents.

If you or your partner come from a family which has a history of inherited disease, genetic counselling before you decide to become pregnant may help you assess the chances of the disease being passed on to your child.

SEXUALLY TRANSMITTED DISEASES

Some sexually transmitted diseases (STDs) can make it harder for you to conceive, and some can be passed on to your baby.

If you or your partner have a sexually transmitted disease, this should be treated before you try to conceive.

About one in eight babies of HIV-positive mothers is born HIV positive too – even if the mother has no symptoms. If you think you might be at risk of HIV, you may want to ask your doctor to arrange for you to have counselling and a blood test before you consider becoming pregnant.

KEY POINTS

✓ Talk to your doctor before trying to become pregnant if you have a long-standing disorder or are on any long-term medication

✓ Wait for three months after coming off the Pill before trying to become pregnant

✓ Start taking a folic acid supplement before you start trying to conceive

✓ Give up smoking before trying to become pregnant

✓ Make sure that you are immunised against German measles three months before becoming pregnant

✓ If there is a history of inherited disease in either family then go for genetic counselling before becoming pregnant

✓ Sexually transmitted diseases must be treated before you become pregnant

How do you know that you are pregnant?

EARLY SIGNS

If your periods are regular, a missed (or sometimes very light) period is usually your first indication that you're pregnant. The signs in the box are some other common signs.

See your doctor as soon as you think that you are pregnant so that you can start having antenatal care in good time.

PREGNANCY TESTS

Two weeks after conception a pregnancy hormone appears in the urine, and a test of the urine any time after this will confirm the pregnancy. The first urine that you pass in the morning is used, because this is when it contains the most hormone. Your GP or family planning clinic will give you a free

SIGNS OF PREGNANCY

- Feeling sick, or even being sick (at any time of day). You may 'go off' certain things that you usually enjoy, such as tea and coffee
- Breast changes – enlarged, tender or tingling breasts
- Feeling tired
- Being constipated
- An increase in normal vaginal discharge
- Needing to urinate more often
- A strange metallic taste in the mouth
- Feeling more emotional than usual

To calculate your expected date of delivery, find the date of the fir
The date immediately below th

January	1	2	3	4	5	6	7	8	9	10	11	12	13	14	15	16
Oct	8	9	10	11	12	13	14	15	16	17	18	19	20	21	22	23

February	1	2	3	4	5	6	7	8	9	10	11	12	13	14	15	16
Nov	8	9	10	11	12	13	14	15	16	17	18	19	20	21	22	23

March	1	2	3	4	5	6	7	8	9	10	11	12	13	14	15	16
Dec	6	7	8	9	10	11	12	13	14	15	16	17	18	19	20	21

April	1	2	3	4	5	6	7	8	9	10	11	12	13	14	15	16
January	6	7	8	9	10	11	12	13	14	15	16	17	18	19	20	21

May	1	2	3	4	5	6	7	8	9	10	11	12	13	14	15	16
February	5	6	7	8	9	10	11	12	13	14	15	16	17	18	19	20

June	1	2	3	4	5	6	7	8	9	10	11	12	13	14	15	16
March	8	9	10	11	12	13	14	15	16	17	18	19	20	21	22	23

July	1	2	3	4	5	6	7	8	9	10	11	12	13	14	15	16
April	7	8	9	10	11	12	13	14	15	16	17	18	19	20	21	22

August	1	2	3	4	5	6	7	8	9	10	11	12	13	14	15	16
May	8	9	10	11	12	13	14	15	16	17	18	19	20	21	22	23

Sept	1	2	3	4	5	6	7	8	9	10	11	12	13	14	15	16
June	8	9	10	11	12	13	14	15	16	17	18	19	20	21	22	23

Oct	1	2	3	4	5	6	7	8	9	10	11	12	13	14	15	16
July	8	9	10	11	12	13	14	15	16	17	18	19	20	21	22	23

Nov	1	2	3	4	5	6	7	8	9	10	11	12	13	14	15	16
August	8	9	10	11	12	13	14	15	16	17	18	19	20	21	22	23

Dec	1	2	3	4	5	6	7	8	9	10	11	12	13	14	15	16
Sept	7	8	9	10	11	12	13	14	15	16	17	18	19	20	21	22

ATE FOR DELIVERY

y of your last menstrual period on the top (bold) line of the chart.
your expected date of delivery.

17	18	19	20	21	22	23	24	25	26	27	28	29	30	31	**January**
24	25	26	27	28	29	30	31	1	2	3	4	5	6	7	Nov

17	18	19	20	21	22	23	24	25	26	27	28				**February**
24	25	26	27	28	29	30	1	2	3	4	5				Dec

17	18	19	20	21	22	23	24	25	26	27	28	29	30	31	**March**
22	23	24	25	26	27	28	29	30	31	1	2	3	4	5	Janu.ary

17	18	19	20	21	22	23	24	25	26	27	28	29	30		**April**
22	23	24	25	26	27	28	29	30	31	1	2	3	4		February

17	18	19	20	21	22	23	24	25	26	27	28	29	30	31	**May**
21	22	23	24	25	26	27	28	1	2	3	4	5	6	7	March

17	18	19	20	21	22	23	24	25	26	27	28	29	30		**June**
24	25	26	27	28	29	30	31	1	2	3	4	5	6		April

17	18	19	20	21	22	23	24	25	26	27	28	29	30	31	**July**
23	24	25	26	27	28	29	30	1	2	3	4	5	6	7	May

17	18	19	20	21	22	23	24	25	26	27	28	29	30	31	**August**
24	25	26	27	28	29	30	31	1	2	3	4	5	6	7	June

17	18	19	20	21	22	23	24	25	26	27	28	29	30		**Sept**
24	25	26	27	28	29	30	1	2	3	4	5	6	7		July

17	18	19	20	21	22	23	24	25	26	27	28	29	30	31	**Oct**
24	25	26	27	28	29	30	31	1	2	3	4	5	6	7	August

17	18	19	20	21	22	23	24	25	26	27	28	29	30		**Nov**
24	25	26	27	28	29	30	31	1	2	3	4	5	6		Sept

17	18	19	20	21	22	23	24	25	26	27	28	29	30	31	**Dec**
23	24	25	26	27	28	29	30	1	2	3	4	5	6	7	Oct

test. Pregnancy advisory services and many pharmacies will also do a test for a small fee. Or you can do the test yourself in private, using a pregnancy testing kit from a pharmacy. Follow the instructions in the pack carefully. If your test gives a positive result you should see your doctor to discuss the next steps you should take.

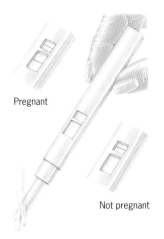

Pregnant

Not pregnant

Home pregnancy testing kit.

WORKING OUT YOUR DUE DATE

The average pregnancy lasts for about 266 days from conception to birth. You are most likely to conceive about 14 days before your period is due. So if you have a regular 28-day cycle you can calculate your approximate delivery date by counting 40 weeks (14 + 266 days) from the first day of your last period, but this is only a guide. A normal pregnancy can be anything from 38 weeks to 42 weeks.

To calculate your expected date of delivery, find the date of the first day of your last menstrual period on the top (bold) line of the chart on pages 6–7. The date immediately below this is your expected date of delivery.

TWINS

Your chances of having twins are about one in 80 – rather more if either you or your partner has twins in the family. Your first ultrasound scan will show whether or not you are expecting twins.

Non-identical (fraternal) twins are three times as common as identical twins. They occur because two eggs are released at one time and are fertilised by two separate sperm. Even if they are the same sex, they will be no more alike than any other brothers or sisters.

Identical twins occur when one fertilised egg divides immediately into two separate cells, each of which develops into a baby. They look alike and are always of the same sex. In the womb they share one placenta (unlike fraternal twins who each have their own placenta).

KEY POINTS

✓ There are certain early signs that commonly occur in pregnancy

✓ Pregnancy tests are available from a number of sources and can be free or involve a fee depending on where they are done

✓ You can calculate your due date by counting 40 weeks from the first day of your last period

✓ Your chance of having twins is one in 80

How your baby develops

THE START OF LIFE

Your baby starts to grow from the moment of fertilisation. But its real development begins about five days later, when the fertilised egg, now a cluster of over 100 cells, reaches the uterus and becomes embedded in its spongy lining.

Fingers from the outer cells of the cluster start to burrow into the lining like roots, linking with the mother's blood supply. These will form the placenta, which will supply all the nutrients the baby needs and carry away all its waste products. Some of these outer cells develop into the umbilical cord, a rope of blood vessels which link the baby to the placenta, and others form membranes that protect the baby. The inner cells form three layers, each of which develops into different parts of the baby's body. The outer layer becomes the skin, eyes, ears, brain and nervous system. The middle layer forms the lungs and digestive system. The third, inner layer will form the heart, blood, muscles and bones.

In only eight weeks this tiny ball of cells will have developed into a recognisable human baby, with limbs, eyes, nose, and a mouth that opens and closes. These early weeks are when the baby is most vulnerable. All the vital body organs are starting to develop and are most easily damaged by drugs or diseases such as German measles.

10–14 WEEKS

By 12 weeks the baby is 4.5 centimetres long. All the internal organs are formed, and most are working, so the risk of damage from drugs or infections is much less. The eyelids have developed, but the eyes are sealed shut, like a newborn kitten's.

The baby can open and close his mouth, frown and purse his lips. Tiny fingers and toes have

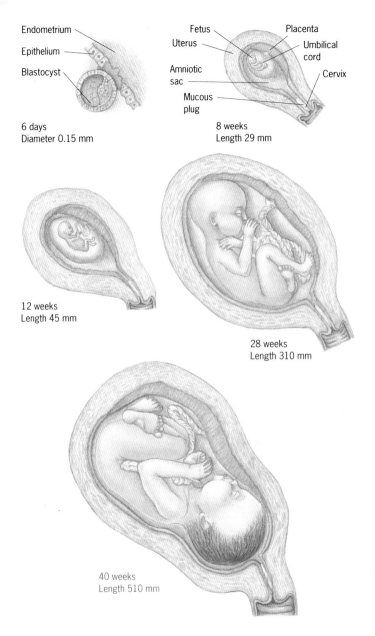

Development of the fetus.

formed, and finger and toenails are starting to grow. The baby can make a fist and curl his toes. The sex organs have developed, but it is still too early to make out the baby's sex on an ultrasound scan. By 14 weeks the baby's rapid heartbeat (about twice as fast as a normal adult heartbeat) can be heard using an ultrasound detector. By 12 weeks you will feel more comfortable in your pregnancy – less likely to suffer nausea or morning sickness. Your breasts will feel heavier and tender. The top of your uterus can just be felt above your pubic bone.

15–22 WEEKS

The baby is now about 16 centimetres long, completely formed and growing quickly. Hair, eyebrows and lashes are starting to grow. The baby can suck his thumb, and grip. Around 22 weeks he becomes covered with fine downy hair (lanugo).

Some time between 16 and 22 weeks you should feel your baby move for the first time. You will look noticeably pregnant by now, but feel less tired and more energetic than in the earlier weeks.

23–30 WEEKS

A baby of 24 weeks is so well developed that he would have a chance of survival if born. His skin is protected by a covering of a greasy substance called vernix.

The heart can be heard through a stethoscope and the baby is now very active, sucks his thumb, drinks, passes urine, and sometimes you may feel rhythmic jerks when he gets hiccups.

By week 28 he can feel pain, and respond to sweet, sour and bitter tastes. By this time, too, he

LIFE IN THE WOMB

Inside the womb the baby floats in a bag of warm fluid called the amniotic sac. This keeps the baby at a constant temperature and protects against bumps.

Even in the womb a baby can hear. If your partner bangs on the side of the bath-tub while you are in it, you'll feel the baby startle and perhaps see it kick. Babies clearly recognise their mother's voice when they are born, as well as music they have heard regularly. They can taste, too, and probably recognise the taste of their mother's breast milk when they are born because it tastes similar to the amniotic fluid they have been drinking in the womb.

will be able to open and close his eyes. By 30 weeks the head-to-bottom length is about 37 centimetres.

These are often the best weeks of pregnancy for you. You will probably feel well and look visibly pregnant, and you may have a 'weight spurt' around this time.

31–40 WEEKS

During the last few weeks of pregnancy fat accumulates beneath the baby's skin and his weight increases by about 25 grams per day. The greasy vernix starts to drop off. In a boy, the testicles usually descend by about week 36. Don't worry if the baby seems less active – he now has much less room for movement. Probably he will have turned into a head-down position, ready for birth. During the last month the baby's head may engage – drop down into the pelvis.

As the uterus expands and presses on your stomach, diaphragm and bladder, you may have some heartburn and breathlessness, and want to urinate more often. During the last month, you will become much more aware of the irregular, painless tightenings of the uterus (called Braxton Hicks contractions), which in fact have been occurring all through pregnancy.

KEY POINTS

✓ The baby is most vulnerable during the first eight weeks

✓ Between weeks 16 and 22 you will feel the baby move for the first time

✓ By 24 weeks a baby is sufficiently well developed to survive if born prematurely

✓ In the last 10 weeks the baby gains weight – increasing by as much as 25 grams each day

Keeping healthy in pregnancy

The placenta is the baby's lifeline. Its rich blood supply provides the baby, via the blood vessels in the umbilical cord, with oxygen and food, as well as the antibodies which will help protect it from infection during the first week of life.

The placenta is a safety net too, preventing the passage of most harmful germs and substances. Unfortunately it is not a complete barrier. Some infections (the AIDS and German measles viruses, for example) can pass through it; so too can nicotine, alcohol and other

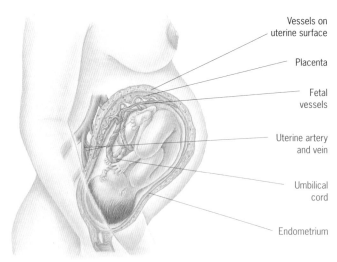

Vessels on uterine surface

Placenta

Fetal vessels

Uterine artery and vein

Umbilical cord

Endometrium

The placenta is the baby's lifeline, supplying blood with nutrients and oxygen and antibodies to protect the fetus from infection, and filtering many harmful germs and substances.

drugs. So, although the baby's natural environment is very safe, you can take extra precautions, maybe even altering your lifestyle a little, to safeguard the baby's health even further.

EATING FOR A HEALTHY BABY

Although it is wise to avoid some foods in pregnancy (see 'What to avoid', on page 17) you don't need a special diet, nor do you need to 'eat for two'. A baby's needs are always met first during pregnancy – if there is any shortfall in your diet, you may suffer; your baby almost certainly won't. Even in the final weeks of pregnancy you will need only about 600–800 extra calories per day.

If you eat a good variety of fresh foods, following the suggestions in the box, and cut down the amount of fatty, sugary, salty and processed foods you eat, you and your baby will get all the necessary nutrients.

You should eat a good variety of fresh foods, cutting down on fatty, sugary, salty and processed foods.

SUGGESTIONS FOR A HEALTHY DIET

- Eat plenty of fresh fruit, vegetables and salads. Cook them lightly or eat them raw. These are good sources of vitamin C and fibre. Spinach and broccoli contain folic acid too
- Make satisfying, starchy foods like wholemeal bread, pasta, potatoes, rice and cereals the basis of your diet. They provide important vitamins and fibre, and don't contain too many calories
- Eat some protein every day. Lean meat or chicken, beans and lentils, fish, eggs and cheese are all good sources
- Eat some calcium-rich dairy products every day – cheese, skimmed or semi-skimmed milk, yoghurt
- Try to eat less sugar and sugary food – these add extra calories to your diet but don't provide any valuable nutrients
- Eat some oily fish such as salmon, trout, herring, sardines and mackerel once a week. These are the richest sources of the long chain, polyunsaturated fatty acids which are vital for the development of your baby's brain, nervous system and retina
- If you are vegetarian, remember that the iron in iron-rich foods such as spinach, black-eyed beans, wholemeal bread, baked beans and pulses is more readily absorbed in the presence of vitamin C. Tea and coffee inhibit iron absorption, so try drinking blackcurrant or orange juice with these foods instead.
- Avoid processed foods which tend to contain a lot of sugar, salt and fat

WEIGHT GAIN DURING PREGNANCY

How much weight you gain during pregnancy will depend partly on how much you weighed beforehand. Most women gain between 10 and 12.5 kilograms (22–28 pounds). If you gain much more than this you'll find it hard to get back to your normal weight after the birth. But it isn't healthy to gain too little weight either.

VITAMIN AND MINERAL SUPPLEMENTS

Every pregnant woman needs to take folic acid tablets (400 micrograms every day) until she is 12 weeks pregnant (see page 2). Otherwise, don't take any supplements unless your doctor prescribes them. If your blood test shows that you are anaemic, your doctor will prescribe iron. If you are vegan and eat no dairy produce, you may also be prescribed calcium, and vitamins D and B_{12}.

SPORT AND EXERCISE

Pregnancy need not stop you taking any sport or exercise that you normally enjoy; however, avoid any activity that may involve contact (blows or falls) or stress to the body, such as riding, skiing and scuba diving. Don't exhaust yourself – you will get more tired than usual, especially in the first and last weeks. Pregnancy is one of the few times in your life when you need rest as much as exercise.

WHAT TO AVOID

While you are pregnant, avoid smoking (and other people's smoke), alcohol, and all drugs and medications except those prescribed by your doctor. You should also take care to avoid certain infections which, though they would do you no serious harm, might cause problems for your baby.

Foods to avoid while you are pregnant.

Make your home a smoke-free zone

You can't afford to smoke if you value your baby's health. If you smoke (or inhale your partner's smoke) your baby is deprived of oxygen, and the more you smoke, the greater the risk to your baby. If you can't give up, at least cut down. There is some evidence that marijuana smoking during pregnancy can affect a baby too.

Babies of smoking parents are more likely to be born prematurely and to have a low birthweight – and this makes them much more vulnerable in the newborn period. Smoking also increases the chances of your having a miscarriage, a stillbirth or a malformed baby. If you or your partner smoke, your child is more likely to suffer chest infections.

And doctors have found that smoking is one of the single most important risk factors involved in cot death (see Reducing the risk of cot death, page 68).

Drinking in pregnancy

Many women find that they simply go off alcohol when they are pregnant; even if you don't, an occasional drink won't do you or your baby any harm.

The problem is that no one knows just how much you can safely drink if you are pregnant. We do know that if you regularly drink two units of alcohol or more every day (one unit is equivalent to a small glass of wine or half a pint of beer) this can seriously affect the developing baby. 'Binge drinking', even if it happens infrequently, is especially harmful. It's best to limit your drinking to no

UNITS OF ALCOHOL

1 unit of alcohol =

1/2 pint ordinary strength beer, lager or cider

or a single measure of spirit or a small glass of wine

or a glass of sherry or other aperitif

more than two units of alcohol once or twice a week.

Remember, a unit is a 'pub measure'. The glass you pour yourself at home may be more generously filled.

Drugs and medications

Most drugs pass into your baby's blood from your own. Some are quite harmless, some (antibiotics, for example) can even be used to treat the baby if necessary, but many can damage the baby, especially during the first three months of pregnancy. Don't take any medicines that haven't been prescribed for you by a doctor who knows that you are pregnant.

It's safest to avoid over-the-counter remedies too, unless you have checked with your pharmacist that they are safe. Paracetamol is safe, as are simple indigestion remedies. Constipation is best dealt with by eating a high-fibre diet. If you are desperate (and many pregnant women are) ask your chemist for a bulking or a stool-softening laxative. These are safe to use because they are not absorbed.

Street drugs must be avoided too. Smoking cocaine or crack, for example, can cause a dangerous drop in the baby's oxygen supply. Babies of heroin-addicted mothers may also be addicted at birth. Avoid X-rays during pregnancy if possible. Make sure that your dentist knows that you are pregnant.

Infections

German measles (rubella) and chickenpox can both be dangerous for your baby. If you have never had chickenpox, it is especially important to avoid it in the final stage of pregnancy. If you catch the disease your newborn baby might develop a severe attack. If you come into contact with either of these diseases and have not had them previously, or, in the case of rubella, been immunised against it, tell your doctor at once.

If you are *not* immune to rubella and come into contact with the disease, see your doctor straight away. Blood tests every two weeks will show whether you have been infected. If so, you will be asked if you wish the pregnancy to be terminated, as infection carries such a high risk of congenital abnormality for the baby.

Many sexually transmitted diseases can affect your baby too, so, if you think there is a chance that you or your partner might be infected, have a check-up so that you can be treated straight away.

Remember that you can get infected by HIV during pregnancy if you have unprotected sex with someone who is infected, or if you use injectable drugs and share needles with an infected person.

If you are HIV positive, there is a risk that your baby will be infected too. You can also pass the virus on to your baby if you breast-feed. If you are, or think you might be, at risk of HIV, ask your doctor for advice and counselling.

Foods to avoid

Listeriosis is a food-borne infection which carries negligible risks for you, but can cause miscarriage or serious illness in a newborn baby. The foods most likely to be contaminated with the organism *Listeria*, and which you should avoid during pregnancy, are those in the box.

Doctors also advise pregnant women not to eat liver or liver products like liver paté or liver sausage. Liver contains a lot of vitamin A, and too much of this could harm your baby.

Animal-borne infections

Toxoplasmosis is an infection which may cause mild, 'flu-like symptoms, but often produces no symptoms at all, and can only be detected by a blood test. However, in a pregnant woman it can seriously harm the unborn baby and even cause it to be stillborn.

So it is safest to avoid anything that might lead to infection while you are pregnant. The organism that causes the infection is found in raw meat and cat faeces.

Toxoplasmosis, listeriosis and an even rarer infection caused by *Chlamydia psittaci*, which causes miscarriage, can be caught from sheep at lambing time. Pregnant women should not help with lambing, come into contact with newborn lambs or milk ewes that have recently given birth.

Peanut allergy

Sensitivity to peanuts can be passed on to your child during pregnancy, while breast-feeding, and in early childhood. Children whose parents, brothers or sisters suffer from allergic conditions such as asthma, eczema or hayfever are much more likely to be sensitive than others. So, if there is an allergy in your immediate family, it is sensible to avoid peanut-containing foods during pregnancy and while breast-feeding.

FOODS THAT COULD CAUSE LISTERIOSIS

- All types of paté
- Soft ripened cheeses such as brie, camembert and blue vein cheeses, goats' and sheep's milk cheese
- Cook–chill meals and ready-to-eat poultry, unless thoroughly reheated before they are eaten

Animal-borne infections.

ADVICE FOR AVOIDING TOXOPLASMOSIS

- Wash your hands after handling cats and kittens, after handling raw meat, and after gardening
- If possible, get someone else to clear faeces from cat litter trays daily. If you have to do this, wear rubber gloves and wash your hands and the gloves afterwards
- Wash vegetables and salads carefully to remove soil that might be contaminated with cat faeces
- Wear gloves while gardening
- Only eat meat that has been thoroughly cooked
- Avoid unpasteurised goats' and sheep's milk and goats' and sheep's milk cheese
- Keep cats off food preparation surfaces

KEY POINTS

✓ Eat a healthy diet

✓ Take a folic acid supplement

✓ Avoid smoking, drinking heavily and taking drugs (whether a medicine or for pleasure)

✓ Try to avoid contact with infectious diseases such as German measles and chickenpox

✓ Be aware of listeriosis and toxoplasmosis and how you can avoid them

Antenatal care

Having a baby nowadays is very safe, mostly because good antenatal care is available for every mother who wants it. Sometimes it can be difficult to keep your antenatal appointments. You may have to take time off from work, or take a restless toddler with you, or wait for a long time if the clinic is busy. But it is worth it to be reassured that your baby is growing normally. If problems arise they will be spotted and can be dealt with straight away. Take the opportunity to ask about anything that is puzzling or worrying you (it is easiest to make a list beforehand of any questions you have).

Most women have their first antenatal check between weeks 8 and 12 of pregnancy – the sooner the better. How often you have antenatal checks will depend on where you live. Most women are given antenatal appointments every four to eight weeks for the first 30 weeks of pregnancy, every two to four weeks until 36 weeks, and then every one to two weeks until 41 weeks.

If you are to have your baby in hospital your antenatal care may be shared between your GP and the hospital. If your GP is to deliver the baby, then most of your antenatal visits will be to the GP's surgery.

Details about your pregnancy, and the results of all the tests you are given, are recorded at each visit in your notes, or on a co-op card, which will be given to you to keep. Ask for an explanation if anything is written which you don't understand.

FIRST VISIT . . .

Your first visit will be the longest. You will be asked a good many questions which may seem irrelevant, but which help the doctor or midwife to discover anything that might affect your pregnancy or your baby. These will probably include the items in the box on page 24.

- Your own and your partner's medical and family history, including your racial origins. This is in case you carry the gene for an inherited blood disorder which might affect your baby. One disorder is sickle-cell anaemia, which mainly affects people of African and West Indian origin and, less often, Indian, Middle Eastern and Mediterranean peoples. Thalassaemia, the other disorder, mainly affects people of Mediterranean and Asian origin. If you or your parents come from any of these parts of the world, you will probably be offered a blood test to see if your baby is likely to inherit one of these disorders.
- Whether there is a history of twins in either your family or your partner's.
- Your previous pregnancies, if any, including miscarriages or terminations.
- Whether you are being treated for any illness at the moment, whether you have any allergies or are taking any drugs.
- What serious illnesses or operations you have had in the past.
- Whether your periods are regular, when the first day of your last period was, and how long your cycle usually is. This helps them work out when your baby is due.
- You may also be asked what work you and your partner do, and about your living accommodation, in case there is anything in your circumstances which might affect your pregnancy.

Weight check

You will be weighed at your first visit. During your pregnancy, you will probably put on 10–12.5 kilograms (22–28 pounds) – more if you were underweight when pregnancy began. You may lose a little weight during the first three months if you suffer from morning sickness. A sudden gain in weight in late pregnancy can be a sign of pre-eclampsia.

General examination

The doctor or midwife will check your heart and lungs and make sure your general health is good.

- **Internal examination:** An internal examination enables your doctor to feel the size of your uterus and estimate your stage of pregnancy. You will be asked to lie on your back with your legs bent and your knees apart. The doctor then puts two fingers of one hand into your vagina and presses your abdomen gently with the other hand. The examination won't hurt, and needn't be uncomfortable if you relax. You will probably not be given another internal examination until week 36.

● **Height check:** Your height, and also the size of your feet, are a good guide to the size of your pelvis. A small pelvis can sometimes mean a difficult delivery. If you are over 152 centimetres (5 feet) tall, you are unlikely to have any problems, unless your baby is very large.

● **Blood tests:** You will be asked to give a blood sample (which will be taken from a vein in your arm) at your first visit, to check the items in the box.

EVERY VISIT
Checking the abdomen
By feeling the abdomen each visit, the position of the top of the uterus can be checked, and this gives a good idea of the rate at which your baby is growing.

Later in pregnancy your abdomen will be felt to check that the baby has turned head-down, and in the final weeks to see whether the head has engaged (dropped down into the pelvis).

Urine test
At your first visit, and then at each visit after week 28, you may be asked for a mid-stream urine sample which will be tested for traces of sugar or protein. Protein in the urine in the last three months may be a sign of developing pre-eclampsia.

You will be asked to wipe yourself with a sterile swab, and

BLOOD TESTS

Blood tests are taken to ascertain the following:
● Your blood group and rhesus blood group. If you are rhesus negative and your baby is rhesus positive, you will be given an injection after the birth to prevent problems for future babies
● Whether you are anaemic (if you are you will be given iron tablets to take)
● Whether you are immune to German measles (see page 19)
● Whether you have a disease such as syphilis or hepatitis B which might harm the baby if not treated

DIABETES AND PREGNANCY

If you have diabetes your doctor will arrange for regular tests on your blood sugar level, and may ask you to come into hospital for the last 10 weeks or so of pregnancy so that the diabetes can be precisely controlled and a careful watch kept on the baby's condition. Uncontrolled diabetes can increase the risk of a baby being stillborn, or of developing abnormally. But if the blood sugar level is kept stable, these risks can be virtually eliminated.

then to pass a little urine into the lavatory before collecting the rest in a sterile container.

Blood pressure

Raised blood pressure in the second half of pregnancy can be a sign of pre-eclampsia (see page 47). However, everyone's blood pressure fluctuates a little – if you have had to rush to the clinic or are feeling anxious, for example, it may be higher than normal. So, if your blood pressure is found to be raised, a second reading will probably be taken.

Hands and ankles

Towards the end of pregnancy most women's ankles are a little swollen

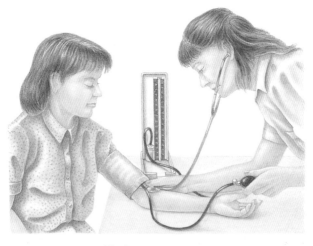

Blood pressure measurement.

by the end of the day. A lot of swelling in the hands or feet can, however, be a sign of pre-eclampsia (see page 47).

Listening to baby's heartbeat

After week 14 your baby's heartbeat can be heard. It will be checked with a 'Sonicaid' which amplifies the heartbeat so that you can hear it too.

Ultrasound scan

Ultrasound scanning is a safe and painless test, which uses sound waves to build up a picture of the baby in the womb. Most hospitals will offer at least one scan during a pregnancy, usually a 'booking in' scan at 11 to 13 weeks to check your estimated delivery date, and an 'anomaly' scan at 18 to 20 weeks to make sure that the baby is growing and developing normally. The baby's sex can sometimes be seen at this stage, but you won't be told this unless you make it clear that you want to know. A few hospitals also offer a special, nuchal fold scan at 11

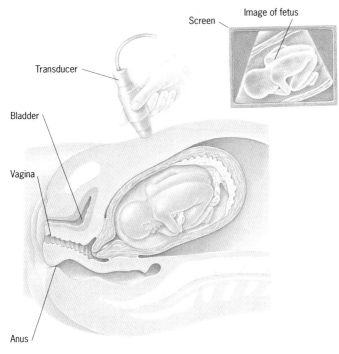

Image of fetus

Screen

Transducer

Bladder

Vagina

Anus

Ultrasound scanning is a safe and painless test, which uses sound waves to build up a picture of the baby in the womb.

to 13 weeks to women aged over 35. This can help estimate the risk of their baby having Down's syndrome. If you have a history of miscarriage, or have had any pain or bleeding, you may be offered a very early scan, at 6 to 11 weeks.

If you are having the test early in pregnancy, you will be asked to drink plenty of water before you come, so that you have a full bladder which pushes your uterus upwards and makes it easier to get a clear picture.

A thin layer of oil is rubbed over your stomach, and a hand-held instrument, called a transducer, is passed gently over it. You and your partner can watch the picture displayed on a small screen, and the sight of your baby moving around inside you will make the baby seem real, perhaps for the first time. Most hospitals will give you a copy of the picture too.

SPECIAL SCREENING TESTS

Some of the tests that you will be offered are to see whether there is a higher than average risk that your baby is not developing normally. If a screening test is positive, you will be given further tests and if it is thought probable that your baby has a serious disability you will be given the opportunity to have the pregnancy terminated.

You do not have to have the tests if you don't want to. But even if you feel certain that whatever the outcome you won't want to terminate the pregnancy, there is still some point in having the screening tests.

The most likely outcome is that they will give you the reassurance every parent wants – that your baby is normal. If not, then you will have time to prepare yourself and your family for a baby with special needs.

Serum screening tests

At 16 to 18 weeks you may be offered a serum screening test. The tests measure the levels of alpha-fetoprotein (AFP) and other chemicals in the blood, and are used to assess your risk of having a baby with spina bifida or a chromosome abnormality such as Down's syndrome.

If you are told the result of the test is positive, it is important to realise that this does not mean that anything is wrong with your baby. All it shows is that there is a slightly higher risk than normal of some abnormality. Usually if you test positive it simply means that the pregnancy is more, or less, advanced than was thought – or even that you are carrying twins. You will be given further tests, such as an amniocentesis, to confirm that nothing is wrong. Almost all of the many women who test positive have perfectly normal babies.

Amniocentesis (14–18 weeks)

Amniocentesis can be used to detect abnormalities such as Down's syndrome or spina bifida. The test involves a small risk of miscarriage (about 0,5 to 1 per cent with ultrasound-guided amniocentesis), so it is not done routinely. But you may be offered it if you are over 37 years old, when the risks of a Down's syndrome baby are higher, or if you have a family history of spina bifida, or if your serum screening test was 'serum positive'.

The position of the placenta is first mapped with an ultrasound scan. Then the doctor inserts a hollow needle into the uterus through your abdominal wall, and withdraws a sample of fluid, which will contain some of the baby's cells.

The cells are tested for abnormality, but it can take three weeks to get the results. The test will also show your baby's sex, but you won't be told this unless you ask.

Chorionic villus sampling (CVS; 10–12 weeks)

This test can detect some inherited disorders (for example, Down's

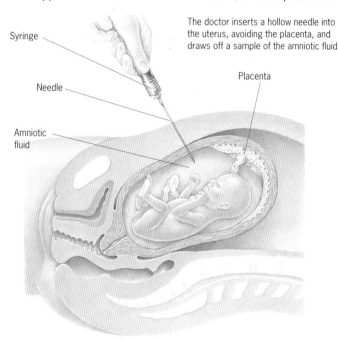

Syringe

Needle

Amniotic fluid

The doctor inserts a hollow needle into the uterus, avoiding the placenta, and draws off a sample of the amniotic fluid

Placenta

Amniocentesis can be used to detect abnormalities such as Down's syndrome or spina bifida.

syndrome, sickle-cell anaemia and thalassaemia) at an early stage in pregnancy – an advantage if the test shows any abnormality and a decision is made to terminate the pregnancy. CVS involves removal of a small piece of the developing placenta, usually by passing a hollow needle up the vagina and into the uterus. The test is painless and takes 10–20 minutes.

It carries a higher risk of miscarriage than amniocentesis (about two per cent), and so will be offered only to women whose babies may be especially at risk.

KEY POINTS

✓ You will be asked a lot of questions on your first antenatal visit

✓ Examination at the first visit includes a general, an internal, a height check and blood tests

✓ At every visit there will be a weight check, a check of the abdomen, a urine test, and blood pressure measurement

✓ Special screening tests pinpoint the cases of higher risk of an abnormal baby; they are not mandatory but can be helpful

✓ You are more likely to be offered some of the special tests if you are 37 or older

Deciding where to have your baby

Most babies today are born in hospital. A hospital maternity department will have an experienced obstetrician on call, as well as all the equipment necessary for monitoring labour and giving emergency care if it is necessary. In some areas you may be able to choose to have your baby in a small maternity unit. It may also be possible for you to have your baby at home.

HAVING YOUR BABY IN HOSPITAL

If you decide to have your baby in hospital, your GP will probably refer you to a maternity unit in the local general hospital. The unit will be headed by a consultant obstetrician, who will have a team of midwives, doctors and nurses under him or her. Unfortunately there is often no guarantee that you will see the same doctor at each antenatal clinic, especially in a large department.

Nor can you be sure which midwife will deliver you. Your antenatal clinics (see page 23) will probably be held in the maternity department at the hospital.

The average hospital stay is about 48 hours, though sometimes it is possible to arrange to be discharged after 12 or 24 hours. But if this is your first baby, or you have had a caesarean section, your stay may be longer, up to 8 or 10 days.

There are advantages in a hospital birth. It can be restful not to have to think about domestic affairs for a while and to be able to concentrate entirely on what is happening to you. And first-time mothers often find the support of staff and other mothers reassuring.

SMALL MATERNITY UNITS

If you live in a small town or a rural area, you may be able to have your baby in a small maternity unit.

A hospital maternity department will have an experienced obstetrician on call, as well as all the equipment necessary for monitoring labour and giving emergency care if it is necessary.

These units are usually run by mid-wives or family doctors, and are not usually available in cities. Such units are more personal and friendly, but do not have the full medical facilities of a hospital.

Your GP and community midwife give you antenatal care. When you go into labour, your midwife goes with you, and delivers the baby. If all goes well you may be able to go home as little as six hours after the birth. Once you are home, the midwife will come in each day to look after you.

HAVING YOUR BABY AT HOME

For a healthy woman, who has had a normal pregnancy and one or two previous pregnancies with no complications, a home birth has no real risks and home may be the ideal place to have a baby. It is usually easier to establish breast-feeding at home and, if you have other children, they may find it easier to accept a new baby if they have been closely involved in the excitement of his or her arrival.

However, you will probably be advised against a home birth if there is any reason to think that your labour might not be straight-forward – if you are expecting twins, for example, or if this is your first baby, because it is impossible to predict what a first birth will be like.

Some GP practices can give maternity care and will attend home confinements. If your own GP cannot do this, find out from the local supervisor of midwives (who is usually head of the maternity services at the local maternity unit) or the Family Health Services Authority (FHSA) in your area which local GPs might be able to look after you. You can then register with this GP just for your maternity care.

A community midwife will visit you to discuss the delivery, share your antenatal care with the GP involved and, usually, she will be the person who will deliver your baby. In some areas, there are independent midwives who special-ise in home births. These midwives do not work for the National Health Service and therefore charge for their services.

MAKING A BIRTH PLAN

Hospitals vary in their routines. It is a good idea to think ahead about the things that matter most to you, and check the hospital policy about them.

Many hospitals encourage you to make out a 'birth plan', setting out how you would like to deal with all the situations that might arise. But remember that you can't predict exactly how you will feel at the time, so be flexible. Even if you don't want to take any drugs, or

QUESTIONS THAT YOU SHOULD ASK

- Can my partner (or a friend) stay with me all through labour?
- Will he have to leave if I have to have a caesarean section?
- Will I be able to move around during labour as much as I want to?
- Will I be able to give birth in whatever position is most comfortable for me?
- Will I have to be monitored, except for medical reasons?
- What percentage of women have episiotomies in the hospital (see page 56)?
- What percentage of women are induced for convenience, rather than for medical reasons?
- What kind of pain relief will I be offered?
- Will I be able to have an epidural (see page 58)?
- Is there free visiting for my partner?
- How long will I have to stay in hospital?
- Will I be able to have the baby with me all the time, or will he or she just be brought to me for feeds?
- Can I feed the baby on demand?

have any medical intervention, make the mental reservation that a very uncomfortable or prolonged labour won't do either you or the baby any good, and be prepared to accept them if it seems the right thing to do *at the time*. In the box on page 33 are some of the questions you might like to ask.

YOUR LABOUR COMPANION

Labour can be a long process, and it can be a rather lonely one unless you have someone to share it with. The ideal labour companion is your husband/partner. But, if you don't have a partner, or if your partner feels the experience is not for him, you may want to ask your mother, sister or a friend to be your labour companion.

ANTENATAL CLASSES

Most hospitals and clinics run antenatal classes which teach both 'parentcraft' – learning how to look after a small baby – and relaxation techniques and exercises which will keep you fit during pregnancy and help you in labour. They will tell you what happens during labour and birth, and how to cope with labour – all of which will help give you confidence if you are at all apprehensive about pregnancy or birth. You will have plenty of opportunity to ask questions and to compare notes with other pregnant women. Nearly all antenatal classes run at least one special session for fathers. Classes are usually timed so that they run for the last eight weeks of pregnancy.

Other organisations, such as the National Childbirth Trust, also run classes for pregnant women. Your local antenatal clinic will be able to give you details of the classes in your area.

WATER BIRTHS

During labour, immersion in warm water can help you to relax and ease pain. The water must be at body temperature – water that is too hot may be tiring for you and may increase your baby's heart rate. Some hospitals provide birthing pools, which are large enough for you to move around in and find a comfortable position, while the water supports your body. It is also possible to hire a portable pool.

You can give birth in the pool if you wish, though the baby must be brought gently to the surface as soon as he or she is born.

If labour has progressed normally and the water is at body heat, your baby won't inhale while under the water. If you want to use a birthing pool in labour, it is important for you to have a midwife with water birth experience.

Water birth.

KEY POINTS

✓ You can have your baby in hospital, a GP/midwife unit or at home

✓ If there is any possibility of problems then it is not advisable to have the baby at home

✓ Make a birth plan which sets out ways of dealing with situations that could arise

✓ Antenatal classes are an important part of the process

Feelings about pregnancy

However exciting it is to know that you are pregnant, and however much you and your partner want this baby, it can be daunting too. Having a baby involves major changes in every aspect of your life. There are practical worries to be faced, about whether you want (or can afford) to stay at home full time, or whether you and your partner should share child-care.

If you stop work, you will lose a whole network of friends and colleagues who have been part of your life. The family may suffer a drop in income too. If you suddenly feel trapped, or occasionally wonder uneasily if you are really ready for such a momentous change, this is only natural.

All these feelings are part of the process of adjusting to having a baby. But the nine months of pregnancy give you time to come to terms with this new stage of life,

and to gain confidence in your own ability to deal with it.

COMMON ANXIETIES ABOUT PREGNANCY

Fear that the baby won't be normal

Almost every prospective parent has this fear at some stage of pregnancy. But the chances of it happening are really very small. Most abnormalities of development occur before 12 weeks of pregnancy and end in an early miscarriage. After this time little can go wrong. Nearly all babies in the UK are born normal and, of those few who are born with some disability, many can be successfully treated. A healthy lifestyle during the pregnancy will reduce the risk even further (see page 14).

Worries about the birth

You and your partner may both have worries about what labour and childbirth will be like, and whether you will be able to cope with the pain. But the more you know and understand about what happens during childbirth, the more confident you should feel. It isn't always helpful to pay too much attention to other women's experiences, because labour varies so much, and people react so differently to it. Use your antenatal clinic and classes as an opportunity to ask about specific fears.

Will I love the baby?

Some women worry that even though they longed to become pregnant, they feel nothing for the baby, and wonder whether they will be able to love him or her. Maternal feelings don't suddenly arise spontaneously during pregnancy. It's difficult to feel motherly until you have something to mother – and even then it's seldom love at first sight.

Your feelings for your baby are more likely to develop gradually as you care for your baby and get to know him or her.

Changing relationships

Pregnancy can never seem quite as 'real' to a man as it does to a woman, who can feel so many changes taking place in her body. It's easy for a man to feel cut off from all the excitement that his partner feels. Jealousy is understandable, too, if the woman is so involved that she gives her partner less attention or affection than he is

However exciting it is to know that you are pregnant, and however much you may want this baby, the prospect can be daunting too.

used to. It's worth making a real effort to spend time together and stay close during pregnancy – remember that for a few weeks afterwards neither of you will have much time and energy for anything but babycare.

Sex and pregnancy

If your pregnancy is normal there is no need to worry that sex might cause a miscarriage or harm the baby. A few women do lose interest in sex during pregnancy, especially during the first and last few weeks when tiredness or nausea tend to dampen down desire. Towards the end of pregnancy your increasing girth may make intercourse uncomfortable in the traditional man-on-top position.

Experiment with other positions, perhaps astride your partner or kneeling with him behind you. Even if sex ceases temporarily, continue to be physically close and cuddle – it will remind you both that you are lovers as well as prospective parents.

COPING WITHOUT A PARTNER

If you are on your own, the normal worries every woman has in pregnancy may seem even more daunting. In these circumstances, friends or family take on a special importance. Even if you've never got on well with your family it is worth trying to build bridges now; you really will need all the help you can get now and after the birth. It is often helpful to meet other single parents too, who have probably had to cope with similar problems.

Gingerbread is a self-help organisation for one-parent families which has a network of local groups, and offers information and advice.

You need not go to antenatal classes alone, or go through labour on your own, even if you don't have a partner. You are entitled to chose anyone you like – a friend, or your sister or mother – to be your labour companion.

If money is your main problem, your local social security office or Citizens Advice Bureau will give you advice. The Citizens Advice Bureau, or your local housing advice centre, can help you if you have a housing problem, too. The National Council for One Parent Families will give you information, and also has some local support groups.

If there really is no one to help you after the birth, it might help to ask your doctor or health visitor if you can be referred to a social worker, or you can contact your local social services department yourself.

They will also help you if you feel you cannot cope with a baby and want to talk about the possibility of adoption or fostering.

KEY POINTS

✓ It is common to have anxieties about abnormalities of the baby, but remember that very few are born with a serious disability

✓ Don't exclude a partner from sharing the time during pregnancy

✓ If you are without a partner, make an effort to meet other single parents

✓ If you have financial difficulties help is available from different organisations

Common complaints

Pregnancy brings many minor discomforts, most of which are at their worst during the first few weeks of pregnancy. Once your body has settled down and adjusted to all the changes of pregnancy, you will feel well and full of energy again.

BACKACHE

All pregnant women have a tendency to suffer from low backache. The extra weight throws out your centre of gravity, and puts a strain on the joints of the pelvis and lower part of the spine, especially towards the end of pregnancy when these joints become softer.

BLEEDING GUMS

During pregnancy the gums become soft and bleed easily, which makes teeth more prone to dental decay. Careful brushing and a dental check during pregnancy will keep your teeth in good condition.

WHAT TO DO TO AVOID BACKACHE

- Keep your back and body straight
- Wear low heels
- Bend your knees, not your back, when lifting
- Use your thigh muscles to push yourself up from sitting. Put both feet flat on the floor, one slightly in front of the other, and lean slightly forward, your hands on your knees
- When getting up from a lying position, roll onto your side, then push yourself up with your arms. If you are in bed, swing your legs over the side and get up as if from a chair

Keep your back and body straight

Bend your knees, not your back, when lifting

Sit with your legs raised and uncrossed

Pregnancy brings many minor discomforts; many can be avoided or their effect reduced.

BREATHLESSNESS

Towards the end of pregnancy you may feel uncomfortably breathless, as the uterus presses upwards on your diaphragm. Once the baby's head engages (page 13) you will have more room to breathe. It will help to use an extra pillow at night – shortness of breath tends to be worse if you are lying flat.

CONSTIPATION

The gut tends to be more sluggish during pregnancy and constipation is often a problem, especially towards the end of pregnancy when the uterus presses on the bowel. Diet is the best solution (see page 42).

CRAMP

Some women tend to get painful cramp in the calves and feet during pregnancy, especially at night. No one really knows what causes it. To ease the pain force your foot flat on the floor, stretching the calf muscles, or pull your toes up hard. Rub the affected muscle, and walk around for a few moments once the pain has eased.

WHAT TO DO TO AVOID CONSTIPATION

- Eat plenty of high-fibre foods, fruit, green vegetables and wholemeal bread, and drink plenty of water
- Don't put off going to the lavatory when you feel the need to empty your bowels
- If constipation is a continuing problem, ask your pharmacist for a mild stool-softening or bulking laxative

DIZZINESS

Occasional faintness is one result of the hormonal changes in pregnancy. You are most likely to feel faint when lying on your back, or if you get up too quickly, or stand for long periods. Sit down quickly if you feel faint, and put your head down. Don't lie on your back, especially in later pregnancy.

FREQUENT URINATION

This is one of the most common and most tiresome symptoms of pregnancy, especially during the first and last weeks.

Unfortunately, there is really nothing to be done about it. If you have to get up often in the night, it may help not to drink too much before going to bed.

HEARTBURN

Heartburn, the burning sensation that occurs when acid juices are regurgitated from the stomach into the gullet, is common in pregnancy. It is at its worst in late pregnancy and when you are lying down. Use extra pillows at night, or raise the head of the bed slightly. Small, frequent meals, and not eating for four hours before going to bed, are also said to help. Don't take an antacid at all in the first 12 weeks, and only take one after this if your symptoms are very troublesome. Then ask your pharmacist for a non-absorbed or poorly absorbed antacid which is safer in pregnancy.

ITCHING

Towards the end of pregnancy, as the skin of your abdomen stretches, it is quite normal for it to feel itchy. However, if you develop very troublesome, generalised itching in the last three months of pregnancy, tell your doctor. This could be a symptom of a rare liver disease, obstetric cholestasis (see page 48).

NAUSEA AND MORNING SICKNESS

'Morning sickness' is often one of the first signs of pregnancy. Although it is often worse first thing in the morning, it can occur at other times, or even all day. Usually it disappears by about week 12 of pregnancy, though you may still suffer occasional bouts later, especially if you are very tired.

It usually helps to eat something dry and bland like a rich tea biscuit when you wake up, then get up slowly. Eat frequent snacks rather than two large meals a day, and don't eat (or cook) anything that makes you feel nauseous.

PILES

Piles are swollen veins around the anus (see 'Varicose veins', page 45) which sometimes develop in pregnancy. They itch, and may be painful or bleed when you empty your bowels. Straining to empty the bowels makes piles worse. If you have always suffered from constipation you may already have a tendency to piles which pregnancy will increase. Mild piles will usually disappear after the baby is born.

But because piles tend to get worse with each pregnancy, ask your doctor whether they should be treated before you become pregnant again.

DIFFICULTY IN SLEEPING

Sleep is often a problem especially towards the end of pregnancy, when it may be hard to get comfortable. Babies often seem more active at night, too. You will probably have to get up at least once in the night to go to the lavatory. In addition to all this, you may wake up feeling hot and sweaty, because the mechanism that controls body temperature sometimes fails to work efficiently during pregnancy.

Don't take sleeping pills, or ask your doctor to prescribe them. A warm bath before going to bed may help you to relax. Try sleeping in a semi-sitting position, propped up with several pillows, especially if

WHAT TO DO TO AVOID PILES

- Eat a high-fibre diet to avoid constipation (see page 16) especially if this is something that you have always tended to suffer from
- Avoid standing for long periods
- Sleep with the end of the bed slightly raised
- Use an ice pack to ease discomfort, or ask your GP to prescribe a soothing ointment
- If the piles protrude from your anus, push them gently back inside

If you sleep on your side, try tucking a pillow underneath the bulge, or under your top bent leg, for support.

heartburn is a problem. If you sleep on your side, try tucking a pillow underneath the bulge, or under your top bent leg, for support.

SKIN AND HAIR CHANGES

The natural pigmentation of the skin tends to darken during pregnancy, especially if the skin is exposed to sunlight – wear a sunscreen with a high protection factor (10–15) if you are in the sun. Your nipples and the area around them will start to darken some time in the fourth month, and so too may freckles, moles or birthmarks. A dark line or pigmented line of skin may also appear from the navel down almost to the pubic hair. Some women develop a 'butterfly mask' – a pigmented area spreading from the nose to the cheeks – in late pregnancy. Most of the abnormal pigmentation will have disappeared within a few weeks after the birth, though if you have had more than one pregnancy your nipples may remain permanently darkened. Hair tends to be greasy, and hair growth increases, during pregnancy. After the baby is born you may seem to be losing a lot of hair, but in fact only this extra growth is being lost.

STRETCH MARKS

'Stretch marks' are red marks which sometimes appear on the skin of the thighs, stomach or breasts in pregnancy. They form if the skin is stretched beyond its normal elasticity, usually because too much weight has been gained too rapidly. Not everyone gets them, but they may be difficult to avoid if you are carrying twins, or if you have naturally small breasts which tend to grow rapidly at the beginning of pregnancy. The marks will eventually fade to less noticeable, silvery streaks, but they seldom disappear altogether. Apart from keeping an eye on your weight, so that you don't suddenly gain a large amount, there is nothing you can do to prevent them. Oiling or creaming the skin won't help.

THRUSH

Thrush is a fungal infection of the vagina which causes a thick white discharge, severe itching and soreness. You will want to urinate frequently, and when you pass urine it stings or burns. Thrush is common in pregnancy, and women who have diabetes are especially likely to develop it.

It is important to have thrush treated before the baby is born, because it can infect the baby's mouth and make feeding difficult. Your doctor can prescribe cream or pessaries (capsules which you insert into your vagina) which should clear it up. To help prevent its recurrence, wear cotton (not nylon) underwear and avoid vaginal douches, deodorant and powders.

TIREDNESS

You may be surprised at how tired you often feel in the first few weeks of pregnancy. By about week 14 you will start to have much more energy again. You will feel able to lead a normal, active life right up to the last few weeks when, as is only natural, you will tire easily and need to rest more often.

VARICOSE VEINS

Varicose veins are twisted, swollen veins that sometimes develop in late pregnancy, usually in the legs and occasionally around the entrance to the vagina. Few women develop them during a first pregnancy, and if they do develop they will improve after the baby is born.

They tend to recur more severely, and to persist for longer, with each pregnancy. Even so, only women who have had several pregnancies are likely to develop severe varicose veins.

Varicose veins are more likely to develop if you gain too much weight, or have to stand for long periods. If they develop try and sit with your legs up when you can – don't sit with your legs crossed. Put support tights on first thing in the morning and wear them all day.

VAGINAL DISCHARGE

It's quite natural for there to be some increase in the amount of mucus produced in the vagina during pregnancy. There is no need to do anything unless the discharge smells unpleasant, is coloured or causes itching. If there is enough to feel uncomfortable use a panty liner or light sanitary pad (not a tampon). Never use vaginal douches; fluid might enter the uterus and cause an infection.

MORE SERIOUS PROBLEMS
Miscarriage

A pregnancy that ends in the first six months is called a miscarriage. About one pregnancy in five ends in a miscarriage, but most miscarriages occur in the first 12 weeks, often before the woman even knows she is pregnant, and usually because the baby is not developing normally.

SYMPTOMS TO TAKE SERIOUSLY

There are a few symptoms which are **not** normal, and may mean that you need medical attention, either immediately or within 24 hours.

If you have any of the following symptoms at any time during your pregnancy, get in touch with your doctor **straight away**:

- Any vaginal bleeding at any time
- Severe stomach pains that last more than a few hours
- Misty or blurred vision in the second half of pregnancy
- A severe headache that lasts for several hours and is not eased by paracetamol
- Pain on passing urine

Get in touch with your doctor within 24 hours if you have:

- Severe and frequent vomiting
- Swollen hands, feet, face and ankles

It is very rare for a miscarriage to occur after an accident or fall unless the pregnancy was so unstable that a miscarriage would eventually have occurred in any event.

A later miscarriage may occur because the placenta is not working properly, or because the cervix is weak and opens up during the pregnancy. Sometimes, if a woman has had repeated miscarriages for this reason, the cervix may be stitched firmly closed at the beginning of pregnancy. The stitch is removed towards the end of pregnancy or when labour starts.

Bleeding from the vagina is the first sign of a miscarriage. If the bleeding is only slight, and there is no pain, the pregnancy can often be saved. Your doctor will arrange for you to have an ultrasound scan (see page 27) to confirm whether the fetus is alive, and to predict whether the pregnancy is likely to continue. Bed rest won't prevent an impending miscarriage, so there is no reason for you to rest in bed unless you feel that you want to.

But, if bleeding is severe or you are in pain, it may mean that the baby has died. You will have to go into hospital so that the contents of the uterus can be removed under general anaesthetic.

Ectopic pregnancy

Sometimes, often because the fallopian tube is blocked, a fertilised egg never reaches the uterus, but becomes embedded in the wall of the fallopian tube and starts to grow there. This is called an ectopic or tubal pregnancy. You will miss a period, and soon after this may have severe pain low down on one side of your abdomen, with vaginal bleeding and perhaps faintness. You will need urgent admission to hospital so that the pregnancy can be removed, and the fallopian tube removed or repaired.

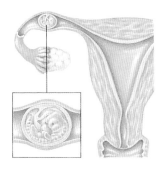

Ectopic pregnancy.

Vaginal bleeding

Bleeding from the vagina can signal danger at any stage of pregnancy. Before about week 28 of pregnancy it can be a sign of impending miscarriage (see page 45). In late pregnancy it may mean that the placenta is bleeding. This can happen when the placenta develops too near the exit of the uterus, where it is more easily damaged (placenta praevia), or if the placenta has started to separate from the wall of the uterus.

The placenta is the baby's lifeline, so if your doctor thinks there is any risk of damage to it you will probably be admitted to hospital straight away. If you have lost a lot of blood you may be given a blood transfusion, and the baby will probably be delivered as soon as possible, by either induction (see page 59) or caesarean section (see page 60).

If bleeding is only slight, and occurs several weeks before the baby was due, your doctor may decide to try to let the pregnancy go to term, while keeping you under close observation.

Pre-eclampsia

Pre-eclampsia is a condition characterised by a rise in blood pressure and swelling of hands, feet or face, which quite often develops in late pregnancy (especially a first pregnancy) though no one knows just why. If you develop any of these early warning signs your doctor will watch you very carefully:

- Raised blood pressure
- Excessive weight gain
- Swollen feet and ankles
- Traces of protein in the urine.

Mild pre-eclampsia is not dangerous, but unless treated it can progress to the much more serious condition of eclampsia, which is characterised by fits and is dangerous for both mother and child.

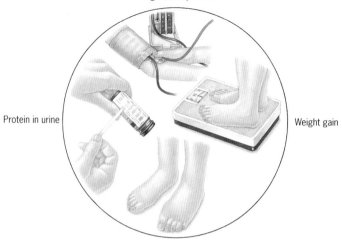

High blood pressure

Protein in urine

Weight gain

Swollen feet and ankles

Pre-eclampsia is a condition characterised by a rise in blood pressure and swelling of hands, feet or face, which can develop in late pregnancy.

At the moment there is no effective way to prevent pre-eclampsia. Bed rest is the treatment often recommended, but there is no clear evidence that it is helpful. If you have severe hypertension, you may be given a drug to lower your blood pressure, and if the signs are severe you may be admitted to hospital even though you may feel perfectly well.

Obstetric cholestasis

This is a rare liver disease which tends to run in families, and may develop during the last three months of pregnancy. Severe, generalised itching is usually the only symptom. If you have very troublesome itching tell your doctor. You will probably be asked to give a blood sample, because liver function tests are the only way to confirm the diagnosis.

As the disease is associated with an increased rate of fetal distress and stillbirth, your baby will be monitored closely, and will probably be induced before your due date.

✓ There are a number of common complaints but foreknowledge can prepare you for them

✓ More severe complaints should be taken seriously and you may need medical attention

✓ More serious problems include miscarriage, ectopic pregnancy, vaginal bleeding, pre-eclampsia and obstetric cholestasis

Labour and birth

How labour begins

Only about five in every hundred babies arrive on the date they are due. No one knows exactly why labour starts when a pregnancy has run its full course. Labour begins in one of three ways.

Regular contractions

This is the most usual signal that labour has begun. Throughout pregnancy you will have felt occasional Braxton Hicks contractions – an irregular tightening and relaxing of your abdomen.

Towards the end of pregnancy these contractions become stronger and more noticeable. When labour begins they start to occur regularly, about every 15–20 minutes at first, gradually growing more frequent and uncomfortable. You may feel these in the lower back rather than the abdomen, but if you place a hand on your abdomen during a contraction you will be able to feel the uterus hardening.

A show

Either just before or at the beginning of labour the plug of mucus which blocks the neck of the womb in pregnancy becomes dislodged and passes out of the vagina, mixed with a little blood. This is called a 'show'.

Your waters break

The bag of fluid surrounding the baby can rupture at any time during labour, but it is less likely to be the first sign of labour than either contractions or a 'show'.

There may be a gush of fluid when they break, though if the baby's head has engaged (see page 13), as is likely in a first pregnancy, there will probably only be a trickle.

When to go into hospital

If your waters have broken you should ring the hospital, and they will probably ask you to come in straight away. Otherwise, unless you live a long way away, there is no need to go in until your contractions are quite strong and occurring about every 10 minutes. Time may go more quickly if you spend the first few hours at home. Keep moving – gentle activity helps labour to progress more quickly. Have a light meal if you can, because you may not feel like eating later on.

Phone the hospital before you leave home.

AT THE HOSPITAL

When you reach the hospital you will meet your midwife and be taken to your room in the labour ward. Here you can change into a hospital gown or your own nightdress.

The midwife will take your blood pressure, temperature and pulse. She will feel your abdomen to check the baby's position, and listen to the baby's heartbeat. You will also be asked for a urine sample.

Between contractions, the midwife may also give you the first of several internal examinations to find out how much the cervix has opened. Once it has opened up to at least three centimetres you will be regarded as properly in labour.

Once all these checks have been carried out, you will be able to have a relaxing bath or, if your waters have already broken, a shower.

WHAT HAPPENS IN LABOUR

A first labour usually lasts an average of 12–14 hours. During the first and longest stage the mouth of the uterus opens up to allow the baby to pass through – this lasts about 10 or 12 hours for a first baby. In the second stage the baby is pushed through the birth canal and is born. This usually takes at least an hour for a first baby, considerably less in subsequent pregnancies. In the third stage the placenta becomes detached from the wall of the uterus and is delivered with a final gentle push.

THE FIRST STAGE

During pregnancy a ring of muscles keeps the long, narrow 'neck' of the uterus, or cervix, tightly closed. Other muscles run from the cervix up and over the main body of the uterus. It is these muscles that contract during labour, gradually drawing the cervix up into the body of the uterus, and widening the opening. Each contraction interrupts the blood supply to the muscle, and causes a temporary shortage of oxygen – it is this that makes contractions painful.

At intervals the midwife will give you an internal examination to see how far the cervix has opened. The cervix doesn't dilate steadily. It may dilate very slowly for a while and then suddenly widen quite quickly. The diameter of a baby's

First stage
Muscles over the main body of the uterus contract, drawing the cervix up and causing it to dilate

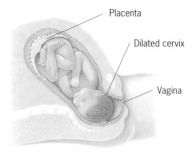

Placenta

Dilated cervix

Vagina

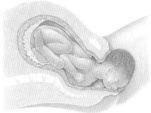

Second stage
Cervix is now fully dilated, and the baby is slowly pushed from the womb out through the cervix and vagina

Third stage
Labour ends with the expulsion of the placenta

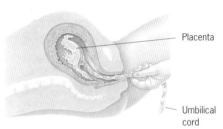

Placenta

Umbilical cord

The three stages of labour.

head is about 9.5 centimetres, and so when the cervix has dilated 10 centimetres it is said to be fully dilated, and the first stage of labour is completed.

Feelings during the first stage

However well prepared you are, the realisation that there is no turning back once labour has begun can be frightening. Your body has been taken over by an unstoppable process, over which you have no control, and which may be more painful than you had expected. Try to relax and 'go with' your body and not fight it. It is at this time that you will most appreciate having your partner, or some other close companion, with you.

Positions for the first stage

You will probably feel more comfortable at first if you move around and stay upright. When a contraction starts, pause and lean forward slightly, supporting yourself on whatever is available – the back of a chair, the foot of the bed or your partner. Try sitting astride a chair, putting a pillow over the back of the chair to lean on. If you do want to lie down, you'll probably be more comfortable on your side than on your back.

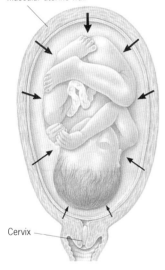

Muscular uterine wall

Cervix

Muscles run from the cervix up and over the main body of the uterus. It is these muscles that contract during labour.

Transition

The most uncomfortable time in labour is at the end of the first stage. The contractions are very strong, and come so quickly that there is almost no time to rest between them. It may feel as though labour is going on for ever. You may be tearful, excitable, or just plain bad-tempered and liable to shout at your partner if he tries to comfort you. You may doze off between contractions, and lose all sense of time. It's quite common to feel sick or vomit at this stage too.

Eventually you will start to feel a strong urge to push, caused by pressure of the baby's head on the rectum. Tell the midwife as soon as you feel this so that she can examine your cervix. Pushing too soon, before the cervix is fully dilated, can bruise it. You can stop yourself pushing by taking two short, panting breaths and then breathing a longer blow out.

Fetal heart monitoring

Each contraction interrupts the blood supply to the placenta. Some babies become distressed during a long or difficult labour, and it is to detect this that the baby's heart is monitored during labour. A change in the baby's heart rate may mean that labour needs to be speeded up because the baby is becoming distressed.

The midwife may use a stethoscope or hand-held Sonicaid to listen to the baby's heart at intervals. Or the heartbeat may be recorded electronically by a monitor which is either strapped to your abdomen or (once your waters

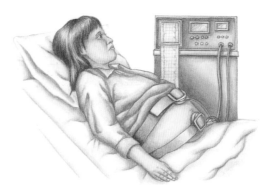

Some babies can become distressed during labour and so to detect this the baby's heart is monitored.

have broken) clipped to the baby's head. The monitor is linked to the recording machine. Some hospitals use electronic fetal monitoring (EFM) routinely throughout labour; others only use it at intervals unless it is felt that there is a real risk that your baby might become distressed. The disadvantage of electronic monitoring is that it restricts your freedom to move around and find a comfortable position during contractions.

THE SECOND STAGE

Once the cervix is fully dilated the active and most exciting stage of labour has begun. Even though the contractions are stronger, they don't feel as bad as in the first stage. You know the end is in sight, and you can do something to speed things up by your own efforts.

As you feel each contraction beginning, take one or two deep breaths, tuck your chin down into your chest and, as the contraction reaches its height, push long and hard. You may be able to push more than once during a contraction, but remember that a long, steady push is much more efficient than several short, sharp ones. Probably you will feel an irresistible urge which will make you want to push at the right time. However, if your baby is lying in a slightly different position you may not, and you will have to push when the midwife tells you to.

Feelings in the second stage

Although pushing is really hard work (every woman will know why it is called 'labour' once she has experienced it), it does not hurt. However, some women find that they are so conscious of the sheer size of the baby in their vagina that they are afraid to push hard, in case they damage themselves. There's no need to worry about this. The vaginal walls are folded and elastic, and stretch easily as the baby is pushed along.

Positions for the second stage

It is better to try to keep a fairly upright position if you can, so that you are working with gravity rather than against it. Most women find a half-sitting, half-squatting position, propped upright with a pile of pillows, is most comfortable. When a contraction comes you can lean forward, holding your knees, to push. Between contractions you can lie back against the pillows to rest.

Squatting is a good position in which to push, but unless you are used to squatting you may find it tiring. A kneeling or on all fours position may be easier.

The birth

With each contraction, the baby's head moves a little further forward, until eventually it is seen bulging against the pelvic floor. The next push may give the first glimpse of the baby's head through the vaginal opening, although, as the contraction dies away, the head may slip back again. Gradually, though, more and more of the head will appear. For a second or two you will feel a burning sensation as the head 'crowns' and stretches the outlet of the birth canal. The midwife will ask you not to push – if the head is forced out too rapidly and under too much pressure, the skin may tear.

So relax and pant, as you did at the very beginning of the second stage. The midwife will try to hold the baby back until the next contraction starts to die away, so that

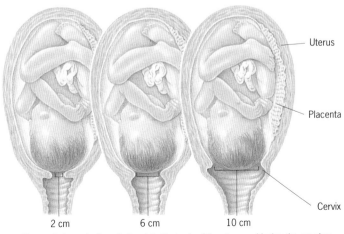

| 2 cm | 6 cm | 10 cm |

The cervix is gradually pulled up into the body of the uterus, widening the opening.

Labels: Uterus, Placenta, Cervix

the head is gently eased through. The next two contractions will push the baby's body easily out.

Episiotomy

Although the skin around the opening stretches easily, it does sometimes tear a little. If the midwife thinks there is a risk of a serious tear she will enlarge the opening with a cut (an episiotomy). After the birth this will be stitched (under local anaesthetic).

The midwife will clear any fluid from the baby's airway, and check that she is breathing normally. You will be able to hold her while the cord is clamped and cut. If you are going to breast-feed, let your baby suckle straight away.

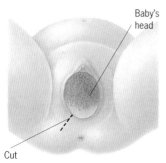

Baby's head

Cut

An episiotomy is a cut made in the skin to enlarge the vaginal opening.

THE THIRD STAGE

Labour ends with the expulsion of the placenta. Just as your baby is born, you will probably be given an injection in your thigh of a drug that makes the uterus contract strongly

and delivers the placenta almost immediately. Less blood is lost if this is done than if you wait for the placenta to be delivered naturally. The midwife may gently pull the cord to help detach the placenta.

The Apgar score

As soon as the baby is born, and again about five minutes later, the midwife will assess her breathing, skin colour, heart rate, movements and response to stimulation, giving her a score (the Apgar score) between 0 and 10. Most babies score between 7 and 10.

PAIN RELIEF IN LABOUR

Some labours are easy, some more difficult, but none is pain free. You will cope more easily with the contractions if you can relax and keep your breathing slow and rhythmic. At the height of a contraction it often helps to breathe in and out through your mouth, taking light, shallow, more rapid breaths.

No one can predict what your labour will be like, so even if you think you would like a 'natural' childbirth, without drugs, you should know what kinds of pain relief are available. The drugs that you will be offered will be perfectly safe for you and your baby.

Gas and oxygen (Entonox)

Entonox is a mixture of oxygen and nitrous oxide ('laughing gas'), which is inhaled though a mask that you hold over your face. It takes the edge off the pain, but won't banish it altogether.

It takes about half a minute to work, so you breathe it in just as a contraction begins. It may make you feel light-headed, sick or sleepy, but if this happens you can simply stop using it. It has no harmful effects on you or the baby.

Pethidine

This is a drug given by injection in your buttock or thigh. It is used quite often, especially in the early stages of labour. Pethidine affects people differently. It makes most women relaxed and a bit sleepy, and lessens the pain a little, while others feel sick, out of control and as though they are drunk. If pethidine is given close to the delivery it can slow down the baby's breathing and make him sleepy.

Meptid (Meptazinol)

This is a drug similar to pethidine, but with the advantage that it has less effect on the baby and so can be given at any stage of labour. You can control the dose yourself via a system that delivers it into your

You will be asked to lie on your side curled up in a ball

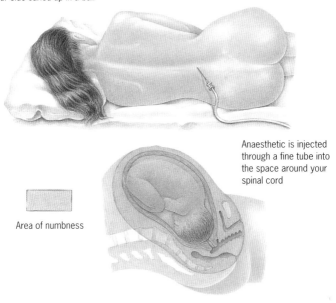

Anaesthetic is injected through a fine tube into the space around your spinal cord

Area of numbness

An epidural anaesthetic is a very effective way of controlling pain in childbirth.

arm. Like pethidine, it may make you sick.

Epidural

Epidural anaesthesia is a special kind of local anaesthetic and a very effective way of controlling pain in childbirth. But it has to be given by an anaesthetist who has had special training, and it is not available in every hospital. If you are interested, check with your midwife beforehand to see whether you will be able to have it.

It takes about 20 minutes to set up an epidural and another 15 or 20 minutes for it to work. It has to be timed carefully, so that you get the maximum relief in the first stage of labour, but the effects have worn off by the second stage, so that it does not affect your ability to push.

You will be asked to lie on your side curled up in a ball, so that your back is rounded. Anaesthetic is then injected through a fine tube into the space around your spinal cord. The tube is left in place so that the anaesthetic can be topped up when necessary.

An epidural has some drawbacks. You won't be able to get out of bed during labour, or for several hours afterwards. You will need to have a drip in your arm and your contractions will be monitored, via a belt round your abdomen. This restricts your movements and may make it difficult for you to get into a

comfortable position. Some women have a headache for a few hours afterwards, and your legs may feel heavy for several hours.

Finally, if the effects have not worn off by the second stage, you won't feel any natural urge to push. The midwife will have to tell you when to push and it may take longer to deliver the baby.

TENS (transcutaneous electrical nerve stimulation)

This method of pain control is only available in some hospitals. It is said to work by stimulating the production of the body's own natural pain-killers (endorphins) through small impulses of electric current. Four electrodes are taped to your back, and joined by wires to a hand-held control with which you can regulate the strength of the current.

TENS is perfectly safe and doesn't involve any drugs. Some women say it reduces their pain, especially in early labour; others find it doesn't help at all. If you are interested in TENS you should practise using it early in pregnancy.

SPECIAL PROCEDURES
Group B Streptococcus

A few women are carriers of a bacterium, group B *Streptococcus*, which can cause serious infection in newborn babies. If you are known to be a carrier, you will probably be given an antibiotic during labour. If it is not known whether or not you are a carrier, you may be given an antibiotic if you go into premature labour, if your membranes rupture before labour begins or if you have a fever during labour, because all these conditions increase the risk of infection for your baby.

Accelerated labour

If labour is progressing very slowly, your doctor may feel that it is best for you and the baby to speed things up. Often simply breaking your waters, if they haven't already broken naturally, is enough to get things moving. This is done very easily and painlessly by snipping the membranes containing the fluid during a vaginal examination. If this does not work you may be given a pessary containing a hormone to soften the cervix, or a hormone drip (see 'Induction' below).

Amniotomy hook

Breaking the waters.

Induction

Sometimes labour has to be started artificially, because there would be a risk to the mother's or baby's health in allowing the pregnancy to continue. This may happen if, for example, you have a condition such as high blood pressure, or if the baby is very overdue and tests show that the placenta can no longer provide the nourishment he or she needs.

After week 40 of pregnancy the placenta starts to lose its efficiency, so that the amount of oxygen it supplies to the baby gradually falls. If the pregnancy is allowed to continue for too long, the baby will only be getting just enough oxygen to keep him or her going. Labour is especially dangerous for such a 'post-mature' baby because, as the uterus contracts, the blood supply to the baby may be reduced even further, to a dangerously low level.

Induction is always planned in advance, so you will be able to discuss it with your doctor or midwife to find out why it is thought necessary. Labour may be started off by inserting a pessary into your vagina which contains a hormone that softens the cervix. Sometimes this is enough to start off a contraction; if not, another hormone, which makes the uterus contract, will be fed through a drip inserted into a vein in your arm.

Even if you know that an induced labour is necessary, you may still feel cheated, especially if this is your first pregnancy.

After nine months of pregnancy it may seem something of an anti-climax simply to go into hospital on an appointed day at an appointed time. But, once labour begins, it will run just the same course as a labour that starts naturally.

Assisted delivery

Sometimes a baby is in an awkward position or is becoming distressed, or the contractions are too weak, or the mother is too exhausted to push any more.

In this case either forceps or vacuum extraction will be used to help the baby's delivery, and unless she has had an epidural the mother will be given a local anaesthetic.

Forceps are only used when the cervix is fully dilated. They fit like a cage around the baby's head so that it can be drawn gently downwards. An episiotomy is nearly always needed for a forceps delivery. With vacuum delivery (sometimes called Ventouse) a small suction cup connected to a vacuum pump is

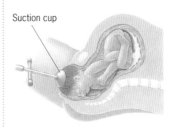

Vacuum delivery.

attached to the baby's head. Both forceps and vacuum cup will leave bruises on the baby's head, but these are harmless and will disappear in a few days.

Caesarean section

A baby born by caesarean section is delivered through a horizontal cut, made through the abdomen and the wall of the uterus, just above the pubic hairline (the 'bikini cut'). It takes only about five minutes to deliver the baby, another 20 or so to stitch the cut. In three to six months the scar will be almost invisible.

You may know in advance that a caesarean section is going to be necessary (an 'elective' caesarean section), perhaps because you have a small pelvis which would make vaginal delivery difficult. Sometimes, however, an emergency arises during labour which puts the baby at risk and makes a caesarean section necessary.

You may be able to have the operation under an epidural anaesthetic, especially if it is planned in

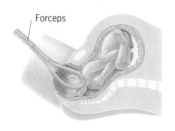

Forceps delivery.

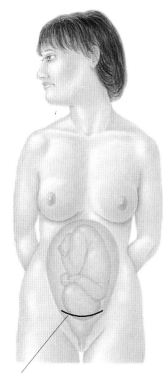

Horizontal cut made through the abdomen and the wall of the uterus

Caesarean section.

advance. You will be awake, though unable to feel anything, throughout the operation and can hold your baby straight away. A screen will be set up so that you do not have to watch what is happening. However, in an emergency there may only be time for a general anaesthetic to be given.

You will be able to walk about soon after the birth. The cut will be painful for a few days, and you will probably have to stay in hospital for at least five days. After about two days the physiotherapist will give you exercises to do to strengthen your tummy muscles. By the time you go home, you will feel much better, though you will need to avoid straining yourself for at least six weeks.

Delivering twins

If you are carrying twins, your doctor will always want you to be delivered in hospital. Twins are often born early and may be small and in need of special care. Quite often one twin is a breech birth, and an assisted delivery may be needed. The babies' heartbeats will be closely monitored, using EFM (see page 54). Usually the second twin is born 10–30 minutes after the first. Sometimes contractions stop after the first birth, and you will then be given a hormone drip to restart them.

Breech birth

About four in every 100 babies are born either feet or bottom first, and this is called a breech birth. Labour with a breech birth is often longer and more difficult, and many hospitals feel that it is safest to deliver breech babies by caesarean section. Some breech babies are born quite normally, although usually an episiotomy and, quite often, forceps delivery are necessary.

Cervix

A baby born either feet or bottom first is called a breech birth.

BABIES WHO NEED SPECIAL CARE

Some babies need special care after birth, usually because they have been born prematurely or are small-for-dates.

These babies may have problems with breathing, feeding and keeping warm, and may need to be nursed in an incubator for a few days. With special care, even babies born as early as 28 weeks can survive.

It is hard to be separated from your baby before you have even got to know her, but you will be able to spend as much time as you like with her and take part in her daily care. Even if she is too small to be taken out of the incubator, you can still talk to her and stroke her gently through portholes on the side of the incubator.

If your baby can suck, you will be able to feed her normally. Otherwise, she will be fed through a tube which is passed through her nose or mouth and down into her stomach.

The baby will thrive best if you express your own milk to give her.

Jaundice

Many babies, especially premature babies, develop mild jaundice shortly after birth, which turns their skin and the whites of their eyes slightly yellow.

This happens because the baby's liver is immature and not yet working properly. Jaundice usually clears up without treatment in a few days, although a few babies need special light treatment. This can usually be given on the post-natal ward.

Jaundiced babies are often sleepy and may need to be woken often to be fed.

LOSING A BABY

Very rarely, a baby is born dead. About 4,000 families a year have babies who are stillborn. Often no one can tell you what went wrong, which makes these stillbirths even harder to bear. It is usually some comfort to see and hold your baby, give him a name, perhaps even ask if you can have a photograph of him. Knowing even this little of the baby makes him seem a real person and easier to mourn. Talking about it to someone who can understand often helps. SANDS (the Stillbirth and Neonatal Death Society, 28 Portland Place, London W1N 4DE; helpline: 020 7436 5881) is an organisation that can put you in touch with other parents who have lost a baby through stillbirth.

KEY POINTS

✓ Labour can start in one of several ways: regular contractions, a show, waters breaking

✓ Labour can be divided into three stages: in the first the contractions bring about dilation of the cervix to 10 cm; in the second the baby is actually born; and in the third the placenta is expelled

✓ Pain relief can vary from gas and oxygen, through to drugs, epidural or an electrical method

✓ Special procedures are used for situations that could be a problem: accelerated labour, induction, assisted delivery, caesarean section or breech birth

The first days with your baby

The first days after the birth should be a time for you to rest and for you and your partner to get to know your new baby. Hold your baby close to you as much as you can. Most babies are more peaceful and settle more quickly when they are held.

Giving birth is thrilling, but it is also exhausting, both physically and emotionally. It will be several weeks before you really feel back to your normal self. You may also have to cope with a variety of aches and pains which make life uncomfortable, although they are quite normal and trivial in themselves.

AFTER PAINS

For a few days you will feel 'after pains' which help the uterus contract and are especially noticeable when you breast-feed. If they are very uncomfortable, take a simple pain-killer such as paracetamol.

When your milk comes in your breasts may feel uncomfortably swollen and tender for a few days. Once breast-feeding is established they will quickly settle down. If you do not breast-feed, your breasts will stop making milk and the discomfort will soon disappear.

SORENESS AND STITCHES

You'll be sore for a few days after the birth – rather longer if you have had stitches. After about a week the cut will heal and the stitches will dissolve, although the skin may feel tight and prickly for a few weeks.

Passing urine may sting at first. If it is very painful, try urinating while sitting in warm water in a bath or bidet. This dilutes the urine so that it doesn't sting.

PILES AND CONSTIPATION

Piles are common after childbirth, but they usually disappear quite quickly. Unfortunately, constipation

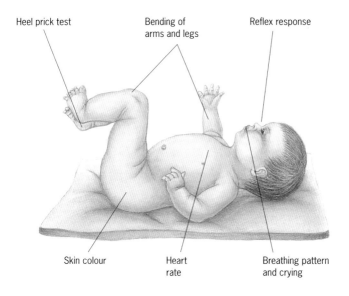

Heel prick test

Bending of
arms and legs

Reflex response

Skin colour

Heart
rate

Breathing pattern
and crying

Check-up of the newborn baby.

is also common, and piles are made worse by painful straining. If piles are very sore your doctor can prescribe a soothing ointment. Eat plenty of fresh fruit and vegetables and wholemeal bread to prevent constipation. If you have stitches, it may feel more comfortable to hold a clean sanitary pad against them while straining to open your bowels.

BLEEDING AFTER THE BIRTH

You will have some vaginal bleeding for two to six weeks after the birth. Wear sanitary pads, not tampons, till it stops. At first the bleeding will be like a heavy period, with some small blood clots (if you pass large clots, tell your midwife). Gradually bleeding gets less and changes colour from bright red to brown, turning bright red again for a while if you are very active. Often the discharge continues till your periods start again.

COPING WITH THE 'BLUES'

Most women feel low a few days after the birth. The sudden change in the body's hormones back to a pre-pregnant state is one reason for the 'postnatal blues'. Another is the normal feeling of anticlimax that tends to occur after any long-awaited and longed-for event.

The blues usually vanish after a few days, but there may still be occasional days when you feel depressed. A baby makes heavy demands on your time and energy. Encourage friends or family to give you an occasional break from baby care. However, if, after five or six weeks, you are so seriously depressed that you can't seem able to cope with, let alone enjoy, your baby, you should talk to your doctor.

SEX AND CONTRACEPTION

For a few weeks after the birth you may be too sore to enjoy lovemaking, especially if you have had stitches. When you start to have sex again, your vagina may be more dry than usual; you may need to use an artificial lubricant such as KY jelly for a few weeks. If you seem to have lost interest in sex this is probably because tiredness or anxiety about the baby means that you have little emotion – or energy – left over for anything else.

Remember that, even if you are breast-feeding, you can still become pregnant again, and so you will need to use some form of contra-ception. Discuss this with your doctor at your postnatal check-up. If you are breast-feeding, some brands of the Pill may not be suitable. An old diaphragm won't fit you properly now; you can be measured for a new one, or have a coil fitted, at your postnatal check-up too.

POSTNATAL CHECK-UP

It takes about six months for the body to return to its pre-pregnant state. But by the time of your postnatal check-up, six weeks after the birth, your doctor will be able to tell whether everything is progressing normally.

THE FIRST DAYS WITH YOUR BABY

Once you are home from hospital a midwife will visit you regularly at home until the baby is about two weeks old. After that, your health visitor will call. She can be a valuable friend, able to advise you about any of the worries that you have in these first weeks. And almost certainly you will have worries – about whether your baby is eating enough, sleeping enough or crying too much.

Getting feeding established

Most babies lose a little weight during the first week. This is normal and doesn't mean that the baby is not getting enough to eat. Whether you are breast-feeding or bottle-feeding, feed your baby whenever he seems hungry – which may be every two or three hours at first.

To make breast-feeding work, do the following:

1. Put your baby to the breast as soon as possible – immediately after birth if you can. Even if it is

Breast-feeding.

only for a short time, this early suckling seems to help establish easy breast-feeding.

2. Let your baby feed as often as he wants and take as much as he wants. Your breasts work on a supply and demand system. The more milk your baby takes, the more your breasts will make.

3. Resist the temptation to top your baby up with a bottle-feed because you think he is still hungry. If you satisfy his hunger this way he will take less from you, and your breasts will produce less milk than ever. Instead, breast-feed more frequently.

During the first days of parenthood you may believe you will never lead a normal life again. But as the baby becomes more settled, and you become more adept at handling him, your life will fall into some sort of routine. Before you realise it you will have slipped imperceptibly from the acute to the chronic phase of parenthood; you will have become a family.

REDUCING THE RISK OF COT DEATH

A very few babies die suddenly and unexpectedly from what is called cot death, or **s**udden **i**nfant **d**eath **s**yndrome (SIDS). Although we don't know why this happens, we do know how to reduce the risks of it happening:

- Always put your baby to sleep lying on his back.
- Keep your baby warm, but don't let him get overheated. Too many clothes or too much bedding is unnecessary if your house is warm.
- Don't smoke, or let anyone else smoke, near your baby.
- Call your doctor straight away if your baby seems unwell.
- Lie him with his feet near the foot of the cot so that he can't slip further down beneath the covers.

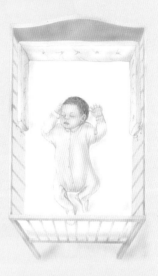

Sleeping position to use to avoid **s**udden **i**nfant **d**eath **s**yndrome (SIDS)

KEY POINTS

✓ You can expect to have 'after pains' and you will be sore especially if you have had stitches

✓ You could well have piles and constipation for a while after the birth

✓ Some women get 'the blues' for longer; if they last more than five or six weeks, see your doctor

✓ Even if you are breast-feeding some form of contraception is necessary if you don't want to become pregnant again yet

Useful addresses

Active Birth Centre
25 Bickerton Road
London N19 5JT
Tel: 020 7482 5554
Fax: 020 7267 9683
Email:
mail@activebirthcentre.demon.co.uk
Website:
www.activebirthcentre.com

ARC (Antenatal Results and Choices)
73 Charlotte Street
London W1T 4PN
Helpline: 020 7631 0285
(10am–5pm Mon–Fri)
Fax: 020 7631 0280
Email: arcsatfa@aol.com

Association for Post-natal Illness
25 Jerdan Place, Fulham
London SW6 1BE
Tel: 020 7386 0868
Fax: 020 7386 8885
Email: info@apni.org
Website: www.apni.org

British Pregnancy Advisory Service
Austy Manor
Wootton Wawen
Solihull B95 6BX
Helpline: 08457 304030 (8am–9pm
Mon–Fri; 8.30am–6.30pm Sat;
9.30am–2.30pm Sun)
Tel: 020 8682 4001
Fax: 020 8682 4012
Email: comm@bpas.org
Website: www.bpas.org

Family Planning Association
2–12 Pentonville Road
London N1 9FP
Helpline: 020 7837 4044
(9am–7pm Mon–Fri)
Tel: 020 7837 5432
Fax: 020 7837 3042
Website: www.fpa.org.uk

Genetics Interest Group

Unit 4D, Leroy House
436 Essex Road
London N1 3QP
Tel: 020 7704 3141
Fax: 020 7359 1447
Email: mail@gig.org.uk
Website: www.gig.org.uk

Gingerbread Association for Lone Parent Families

7 Sovereign Court
Sovereign Close
London E1W 3HW
Adviceline: 0800 0184318
(10am–4pm Mon–Fri)
Tel: 020 7488 9300
Fax: 020 7488 9333
Email: office@gingerbread.org.uk
Website: www.gingerbread.org.uk

Hysterectomy Support Network

For information about this and other
related issues, contact:
Women's Health
52 Featherstone Street
London EC1Y 8RT
Helpline: 020 7251 6580 (Mon–Fri
9.30am–1.30pm)
Fax: 020 7608 0928
Minicom: 020 7490 5489
Email:
health@womenshealthlondon.org.uk
Website:
www.womenshealthlondon.org.uk

Maternity Alliance

(help with rights and benefits)
45 Beech Street
London EC2P 2LX
Information line: 020 7588 8582
(10.30am–12.30pm Mon–Thu (not
Tues); 6pm–8pm Tue)
Fax: 020 7588 8584
Email:
info@maternityalliance.org.uk
Website:
www.maternityalliance.org.uk

Miscarriage Association

c/o Clayton Hospital
Northgate
Wakefield
West Yorkshire WF1 3JS
Helpline: 01924 200799 (Mon–Fri
9am–4pm)
Fax: 01924 298834
Email:
miscarriageassociation@care4free.net
Website:
www.miscarriageassociation.org.uk

National Childbirth Trust

Alexandra House
Oldham Terrace
London W3 6NH
Tel: 08704 448707 (9.30–4.30
Mon–Fri)
Fax: 020 8992 5929
Website: www.nct-online.org

National Council for One Parent Families

255 Kentish Town Road
London NW5 2LX
Helpline: 0800 018 5026
Fax: 020 7482 4851
Email:
info@oneparentfamilies.org.uk
Website:
www.oneparentfamilies.org.uk

Parentline Plus

520 Highgate Studios
53–79 Highgate Rd
Kentish Town
London NW5 1TL
Helpline: 0808 800 2222
(9am–9pm Mon–Fri; 9am–5pm Sat;
10am–3pm Sun)
Textphone: 0800 783 6783
Tel: 020 7284 5500
Email:
centraloffice@parentlineplus.org.uk
Website:
www.parentlineplus.org.uk

Quit

(advice on giving up smoking)
Victory House
170 Tottenham Court Rd
London W1P 0HA
Tel: 020 7388 5775
Fax: 020 7388 5995
Email: quit-projects@clara.co.uk
Website: www.quit.org.uk

Smoking Quitlines

England: 0800 002200
(Additional support available
during pregnancy and the post-
natal period)
N. Ireland: 028 9066 3281
Scotland (Smokeline): 0800
848484
Wales: 0345 697500

SANDS (Stillbirth and Neonatal Death Society)

28 Portland Place
London W1B 1LY
Helpline: 020 7436 5881
(10am–3.30pm Mon–Wed)
Tel: 020 7436 7940
Fax: 020 7436 3715
Email: support@uk-sands.org
Website: www.uk-sands.org

Index